D0363694

GO FACTS NATURAL ENVIRONMENTS
Mountains

A & C BLACK • LONDON

Mountains

HERTFORDSHIRE LIBRARIES	
H45 703 646 8	
PET	05-Jan-2009
C577.5	£8.99
9781408104798	

Copyright © 2007 Blake Publishing
Additional material © A & C Black Publishers Ltd 2008

First published in Australia by Blake Education Pty Ltd

This edition published in the UK in 2008 by
A & C Black Publishers Ltd, 38 Soho Square, London. W1D 3HB
www.acblack.com

Published by permission of Blake Publishing Pty Ltd, Leichhardt NSW, Australia. All rights reserved. No part of this publication may be reproduced in any form or by any means – graphic, electronic or mechanical, including photocopying, recording, taping or information storage and retrieval systems - without the prior written permission of the publishers.

Hardback edition
ISBN 978-1-4081-0479-8

Paperback edition
ISBN 978-1-4081-0480-4

A CIP record for this book is available from the British Library.

Author: Ian Rohr
Publisher: Katy Pike
Editor: Mark Stafford
Design and layout by The Modern Art Production Group

Image credits: p13 (all) – Mark Stafford; p17 (bottom right) – Fredy Mercay/ANTPhoto.com
Printed in China by WKT Company Ltd.

This publication is produced using paper that is made from wood grown in managed sustainable forests. It is natural, renewable and recyclable. The logging and manufacturing processes conform to the environmental regulations of the country of origin.

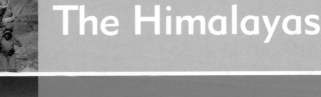

What are Mountains?

Mountains rise above the landscape. Many have steep, sloping sides that form a **peak**. Some mountains stand by themselves. Others are part of mountain ranges.

Mountain heights are measured by the number of metres above sea level. A mountain has different environments based on **altitude**. There are different weather conditions and types of plants and animals at different heights on the mountain. As you go up a large mountain, the environment can change from jungle to grassland to rocky peak.

The **snow line** is the height above which there is always snow.

Conditions become harsher the higher you climb. The air gets thinner because there is less oxygen. Thin air is cold. The temperature drops about 1 °C (1.8 °F) for every 150 metres you climb.

The world's tallest mountains are part of ranges.

The Matterhorn in Switzerland

GO FACT!

THE HIGHEST

Mount Everest is the highest mountain in the world. It is 8848 metres above sea level.

Mountain weather changes quickly.

Mountains of the World

Mountains are created by enormous forces within the Earth.

Mountains form when **tectonic plates** collide. Tectonic plates are the large, moving plates of land that make up the Earth's surface. Volcanic activity also creates mountains.

Fold mountains are the tallest mountains in the world. The collision of tectonic plates forces huge amounts of rock to fold and move upwards. This makes long, high mountain ranges, such as the Alps, Himalayas and Russia's Urals.

Mount Garibaldi in Canada is an eroded dome mountain.

Block mountains, including Mount Kilimanjaro in Africa, are created at cracks in the Earth's surface. Large blocks of rock are pushed upwards.

Volcanic activity creates dome mountains as **lava** pushes up from beneath the Earth's surface. This produces round mountains, such as the Adirondack Mountains in the USA. Dome mountains **erode** into peaks and valleys.

The Flinders Ranges in South Australia are block mountains.

The Rockies that run through the USA and Canada form a fold mountain range.

GO FACT!

THE LONGEST

The world's longest mountain range is the Andes. It runs the whole length of South America.

Mount Fuji in Japan is an isolated mountain produced by a volcano.

7

Mountains are always eroding. This is mainly due to the effects of ice, rain and wind.

At the tops of mountains, water freezes in cracks in the rock. The water expands when it freezes. It causes the rock to split and pieces break off. This makes mountains jagged.

Rivers and **glaciers** move tonnes of rock and soil, carving out mountain valleys.

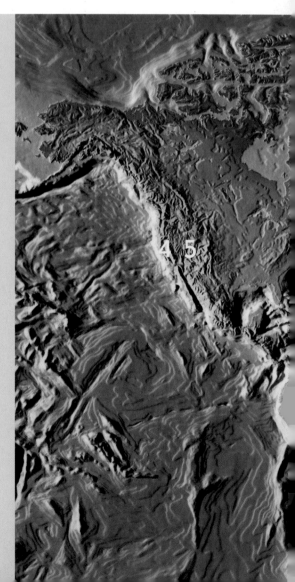

Mountain Ranges of the World

1 The Eastern Highlands

2 The Southern Alps

3 Mount Fuji

4 The Sierra Nevada

5 The Rockies

6 The Andes

7 The Atlas Mountains

8 The Central African Highlands

9 The Pyrenees

10 The Urals

11 The Alps

12 The Carpathians

13 The Himalayas

Athabasca Glacier, Canada

The Himalayas

The highest mountain range on Earth is the Himalayas. It runs through India, Pakistan, Nepal, Bhutan and China.

The Himalayan mountain range was formed when the Indian tectonic plate crashed into Asia. This happened about 70 million years ago.

Mount Everest

The environment is tropical at the bottom of the Himalayas. At the top it is rock, snow and ice. Many peaks are above the clouds most of the time.

There are two main seasons. There is a short, cool summer and a long, cold winter. People living in the mountains have larger lungs than other people. This helps them get enough oxygen from the thin air.

The 14 highest mountains in the world are in the Himalayas.

The Himalayan snow leopard is a rare big cat.

GO FACT!

THE FIRST

The first people to climb Mount Everest in the Himalayas were Tenzing Norgay and Sir Edmund Hillary in 1953. Sir Edmund's son, Peter, also climbed Everest, in 1990.

A village in Nepal

Make a Mountain Range

Make your own fold mountain range.

You will need:

- modelling clay in three different colours
- a rolling pin, ruler and blunt knife
- two square blocks of wood, about five centimetres wide
- two rectangular blocks of wood, about ten centimetres long and five centimetres wide

1 Roll out the clay into sheets about one centimetre thick. Make each sheet the same size.

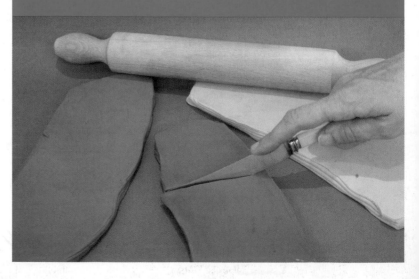

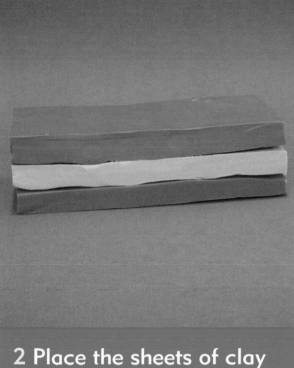

2 Place the sheets of clay on top of each other.

3 Place the rectangular blocks either side of the sheets of clay. Put the square blocks at each end.

4 Ask a friend to hold on to the block at one end while you push the other towards it.

Result The layers fold and crumple. This is what happens to rocks when tectonic plates collide.

13

Mountain Plants

Different plants live at different altitudes on a mountain.

The lower slopes of a mountain have trees, shrubs and flowering plants. The higher slopes have mostly small flowering plants, such as daisies and marigolds.

The **tree line** is the height above which it is too cold and windy for trees to grow. Most trees and shrubs near the tree line are short and grow slowly.

Above the tree line, grasses and flowers grow close to the ground. These plants grow slowly because the soil is sandy and rocky. They make as much food as possible during the short summer. They store this food in their roots for winter.

Bog plants, such as moss and heath, also grow above the tree line.

Oak leaves and acorns

14

Snow gums grow at the tree line in Australia.

There are lots of grasses and flowers above the tree line.

Spring gentian

Mountain Animals

Like plants, different animals live at different altitudes on a mountain.

An animal on one part of a mountain may never see the other animals living above or below it on the mountain.

Animals that live at high altitudes adapt to cope with the harsh environment. They have short tails and ears to reduce heat loss from their bodies. Some have thick layers of fat and fur to stay warm. Smaller animals often live in burrows, where it is warmer.

Grey wolf

Large animals, like mountain goats, are good climbers, which means they can travel over steep rocks. The snowshoe hare has brown fur in summer. In winter it turns white, so **predators** can't see it in the snow.

At the start of winter, some animals, such as bighorn sheep, move down the mountain to where it is warmer and there is more food.

Yaks are used to supply milk and meat and to carry things.

Snowshoe hare

Australia's mountain pygmy possum is very rare.

17

Surviving the Cold

Some animals survive winter on a mountain by **hibernating**. This means they sleep through the coldest months, living on food they have stored.

Black bears in the mountains of North America hibernate every winter.

1 The bear eats as much as possible in summer and autumn.

2 In winter, when there is not much food left, the bear goes into a den to sleep. The den might be a cave, burrow, or the space under some logs on the ground.

3 The bear's breathing rate drops. It can be as slow as one breath every 45 seconds. It sleeps for four to seven months.

4 The bear comes out of the den in spring.

Avalanche!

An avalanche is a mass of snow, rock or soil sliding down a mountain.

A snow avalanche occurs when a weak layer of snow slips. The layers of snow then slide down the mountain.

An avalanche can be triggered by a falling tree, a change in the weather, or by someone skiing or hiking. People also start small avalanches on purpose to avoid lots of snow building up.

Avalanches travel at great speeds. They can crash down onto people and towns. In 1970, an earthquake started an avalanche of snow and rock in Peru. It buried two towns and killed 18 000 people.

Saint Bernard dogs can smell people trapped under snow.

Rescue teams help people hurt by avalanches.

An avalanche in Switzerland

A dangerous build-up of snow

GO FACT!

THE FASTEST

The fastest avalanche recorded was on Mount St Helens, Washington USA. The mountain erupted and started a rock avalanche that reached 402 kilometres per hour.

Does It Hibernate?

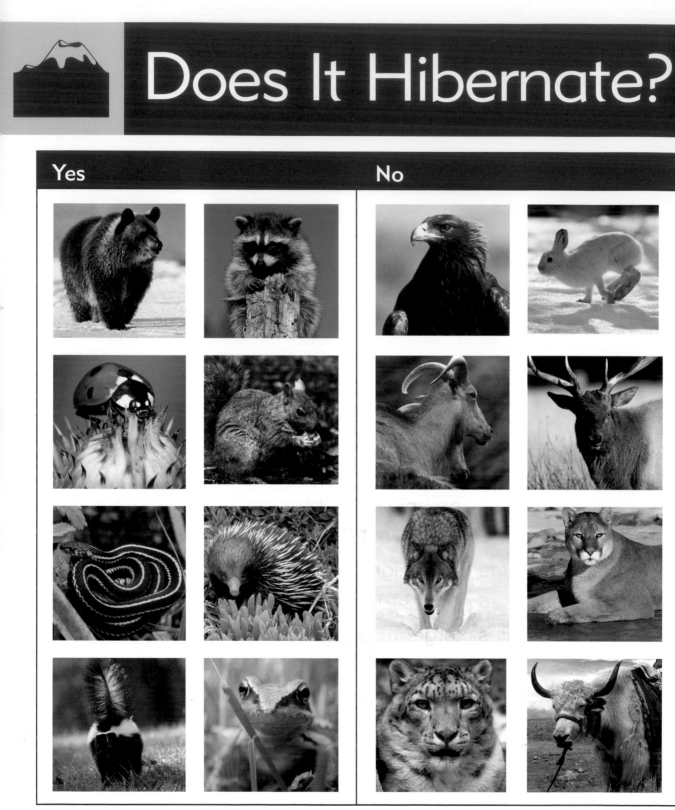

Yes

No

Glossary

altitude	height above sea level
erode	to wear away at the Earth's surface by water, wind and ice
glacier	a slowly moving body of ice, made by the build-up of snow
hibernate	to spend the winter sleeping
lava	hot, liquid rock which comes out of the Earth
peak	the pointed top of a mountain, or the mountain itself
predator	an animal that hunts, kills and eats other animals
snow line	the height on a mountain above which there is always snow
tectonic plates	large, thick plates of land that move very slowly across the Earth's surface
tree line	the height on a mountain above which there are no trees

# Index